Table of Contents

Welcome

Have you ever said to yourself, "I want to become a best-selling artist, author musician," or whatever else your chosen craft is? I am guessing if you're reading this book, you probably have. I am also guessing that you may have heard many horror stories of how hard it is to make a success with your art business. Don't get me wrong, it is much harder to become a success in this day and age than it ever has been, and yet at the same time, it's actually easier than ever before.

Becoming a successful artist whether that's as a musician, author, painter, sculptor, sketcher, or whatever you may be is the same today as it was 200 years ago. The core elements and key ingredients haven't changed. It is all about selling a product that we have invested time, love and energy into and selling it to somebody who loves all your efforts.

When you get to the heart of the things, however difficult this may be for you to believe, selling a painting, selling a song, selling a book, is no different than selling software, selling windows, or selling tarmac, they are all products and all have an audience who will pay money for them.

Now my guessing is if you're reading this, you're excited about the prospect of becoming a best-selling author, or an internationally renowned artist, or even an amazing musician. This adventurous spirit is within you for a reason, and it is prompting you to take action.

Over the last 20 years, I have personally ventured in and out of all three of these industries and more, and had great success and enjoyed them tremendously.

While I'm not up there with Justin Bieber or Ed Sheeran, I do have a very loyal following that have followed and supported me and my work over the last 20 years. It is crafting a loyal following that I want to make the emphasis of this little book.

When an audience loves you, your artwork and follows along your journey, it is one of the most amazing things that a human being can ever experience. Your audience wants you to succeed. Your audience wants you to do well, and building relationships with them is one of the best things that you can do.

So if this sounds like you, and if you want to be a success at what you do, and you want to make a living with your chosen skill, then this book is for you.

This book has been compiled from the 20 years' experience which I have personally learned and found to be beyond measure in its value level.

In this book you shall learn all about: Getting started, marketing, sales, building relationships, websites, SEO, product lines, social media and what it does and so much more.

This book is for creative minds and has been written by a very creative mind. So here we go, hand in hand, ready to begin the adventure together...

Here's to your success,

John

Chapter 1 The creative industry...

The creative industry is a rapidly growing field, with a wide range of opportunities for entrepreneurs looking to start their own business. Whether you are an artist, designer, writer, musician, or any other type of creative professional, there are many challenges to overcome when starting and running a creative business. In this section, we will explore the key steps and strategies for setting up and running a creative business successfully.

Setting up a Creative Business: Develop a Business Plan Before starting your creative business, it is essential to develop a comprehensive business plan. A business plan is a detailed roadmap for your business that outlines your goals, strategies, target audience, marketing plan, and financial projections. A well-crafted business plan will help you to define your business model, identify potential challenges, and create a plan to overcome them.

Define Your Brand Identity:
Your brand identity is a critical aspect of your creative business. It defines who you are, what you stand for, and how you communicate with your target audience. To define your brand identity, you need to develop a brand name, logo, colour scheme, and brand messaging that reflects your creative vision and resonates with your target audience.

Create a Portfolio of Your Work A portfolio of your work is an essential component of your creative business. Your portfolio should showcase your best work and highlight your unique style, creative vision, and areas of expertise. Your portfolio can be in the form of a website, social media page, or physical portfolio, depending on your business needs.

Establish a Legal Structure:
Establishing a legal structure is crucial when starting a creative business. This involves choosing the legal entity that best suits your business needs, registering your business, obtaining necessary licenses and permits, and setting up accounting and tax systems.

Running a Creative Business: Build a Strong Online Presence A strong online presence is critical for the success of a creative business. Your website, social media, and other online platforms can help you to reach a broader audience, showcase your work, and connect with potential clients. It is essential to create a consistent online brand identity across all platforms and engage with your followers regularly.

Develop Strong Relationships with Clients:

Developing strong relationships with clients is essential for the success of a creative business. This involves building trust, communicating effectively, and providing high-quality work that meets their needs. It is also essential to provide excellent customer service and follow up with clients after completing a project to ensure their satisfaction.

Market Your Business Effectively:

Marketing is a crucial aspect of running a creative business. Effective marketing involves understanding your target audience, identifying the most effective marketing channels, and developing a marketing plan that aligns with your business goals. It is also essential to track the effectiveness of your marketing efforts and adjust your strategies accordingly.

Continuously Develop Your Skills and Expertise:

The creative industry is constantly evolving, and it is essential to stay up-to-date with the latest trends, technologies, and industry best practices. Continuously developing your skills and expertise will help you to stay competitive, offer high-quality work, and provide value to your clients. Conclusion: Starting and running a creative business can be a challenging task, but by following the steps and strategies outlined in this book, you can increase your chances of success. By developing a comprehensive business plan, defining your brand identity, creating a portfolio of your work, and establishing a legal structure, you can set your business up for success.

Choosing a name for your business...

The importance of choosing a good name for your art business cannot be overstated. The name of your art business is one of the most critical components of its brand identity, and it can have a significant impact on its success and longevity. A well-chosen name can help create a strong brand identity, build customer loyalty, and establish a positive reputation in the industry. On the other hand, a poorly chosen name can hinder the growth of the business, confuse customers, and even lead to legal problems.

In this section, we will explore the reasons why choosing a good name is essential, the benefits of having a strong brand identity, and provide some tips on how to come up with an effective name. Why Choosing a Good Name Is Important Brand Identity Your art business's name is one of the most critical components of its brand identity. A well-chosen name can create a memorable and recognizable brand that sets your business apart from competitors. Your name should reflect the type of art your business produces, as well as its unique style and personality. For example, a business that produces contemporary abstract art may want to choose a name that reflects this style, such as "Brushstrokes" or "Canvas Dreams." Customer Loyalty A good name can also help build customer loyalty. Customers are more likely to return to a business with a memorable and positive name.

A catchy name that is easy to remember can help customers recall your business and recommend it to others. A name that reflects your business's values and mission can also help create a connection with customers. For example, a business that focuses on promoting local artists may choose a name that reflects this, such as "Artisan Alley." Reputation Your art business's name can also influence its reputation in the industry. A name that is generic, confusing, or offensive can damage your business's reputation and turn away potential customers.

On the other hand, a name that is unique, creative, and professional can help establish a positive reputation. A name that is easy to spell and pronounce can also make it easier for customers to find and remember your business. For example, a business that produces handmade jewellery may choose a name that reflects this, such as "Crafted Creations." Legal Issues Choosing a name for your art business is not just a creative process. It also involves legal considerations. Your business name must be original and not infringe on another business's trademark. It is essential to conduct a thorough search to ensure that the chosen name is available and not already in use by another business. Failing to do so can result in legal problems and costly legal battles. For this reason, it is advisable to consult a lawyer or a legal professional to help ensure that the chosen name is legally sound.

The Benefits of Having a Strong Brand Identity:
A strong brand identity can have many benefits for your art business. It can

help you stand out in a crowded market, build customer loyalty, and establish a positive reputation in the industry. Here are some of the key benefits of having a strong brand identity:

Recognition: A strong brand identity can help your art business stand out in a crowded market. When customers see your logo or business name, they should be able to recognize your brand immediately. This can help build brand recognition and make it easier for customers to find and remember your business.

Customer Loyalty:

A strong brand identity can also help build customer loyalty. When customers feel a connection to your brand, they are more likely to return to your business and recommend it to others. A well-designed logo and consistent branding can help create a sense of trust and familiarity with customers, which can help build loyalty over time.

Credibility:

A strong brand identity can also help establish your business's credibility in the industry. When customers see a well-designed logo and consistent branding, it can convey a sense of professionalism and expertise. This can help establish your business as a trusted and reliable source of quality art products and services.

Differentiation:

A strong brand identity can also help differentiate your business from competitors. When customers can easily recognize and remember your brand, it can set your business apart from others in the industry. A unique and creative name and logo can help make your business more memorable and distinctive, which can help attract new customers and retain existing ones. Brand Value: Finally, a strong brand identity can increase the overall value of your art business. A well-established brand can be a valuable asset, as it can create a positive reputation and help build customer loyalty. This can translate into increased sales, higher profits, and a stronger market position in the industry.

Tips for Choosing a Good Name for Your Art Business:

Choosing a good name for your art business is a crucial step in establishing a strong brand identity. Here are some tips to help you come up with an effective name: Consider Your Brand Identity Before choosing a name, consider your brand identity and the type of art your business produces. Your name should reflect your business's unique style and personality.

It should also be easy to remember and recognize. Consider the type of art your business produces, as well as your target audience and the image you want to convey. Make It Unique A unique name can help set your art business apart from competitors. Avoid generic names that may be confusing or easily forgotten. Instead, try to come up with a name that is distinctive, creative, and memorable. Consider using a play on words, a pun, or a creative twist on a common phrase or expression.

Keep It Simple Your business name should be easy to spell and pronounce. Avoid using complicated words or long phrases that may be difficult to remember or spell. Keep it simple, straightforward, and easy to recognize. Conduct a Search Before finalizing your business name, conduct a thorough search to ensure that it is not already in use by another business. This can help you avoid legal issues and conflicts down the road. You can conduct a search on the US Patent and Trademark Office website or consult a legal professional for assistance. Test It Out Once you have come up with a list of potential names, test them out with friends, family, and potential customers. Get feedback on which names are memorable, easy to remember, and effective in conveying your business's brand identity. This can help you narrow down your choices and choose the best name for your art business.

In conclusion, choosing a good name for your art business is an essential step in establishing a strong brand identity. A well-chosen name can create a memorable and recognizable brand, build customer loyalty, and establish a positive reputation in the industry. On the other hand, a poorly chosen name can hinder the growth of the business, confuse customers, and even lead to legal problems. To choose an effective name for your art business, consider your brand identity, make it unique, keep it simple, conduct a search, and test it out. By following these tips, you can choose a name that reflects your business's unique style and personality, sets it apart from competitors, and helps build a positive reputation in the industry.

Chapter 2 Your niche.

Introduction: Starting an art business can be a daunting task. The art industry is vast and diverse, with different sectors ranging from fine arts to commercial arts. Therefore, understanding your art business niche is essential. Your niche is the specific area of the art industry that you specialize in or focus on. Identifying your niche will help you understand your target audience, build your brand identity, and create a sustainable business model.
Understanding Your Art Business Niche:

Fine Art:
The Fine art sector involves creating original artworks, such as paintings, sculptures, and installations, and selling them directly to collectors, galleries, or museums. Artists in this sector usually work independently, creating pieces that reflect their unique style and artistic expression. They often exhibit their work in galleries and at art fairs. To succeed in the fine art sector, artists must be innovative and have a distinct style that stands out in the market. They should also have strong marketing skills and the ability to build relationships with collectors and galleries.

Commercial Art:
 The commercial art sector involves creating art for commercial purposes, such as advertising, packaging, book covers, and other marketing materials. Artists in this sector often work for advertising agencies, design firms, and publishing houses. They are required to create artwork that meets the specific needs and objectives of the client. To succeed in the commercial art sector, artists must have a good understanding of the client's brand identity and objectives. They must also be able to work efficiently and meet tight deadlines while producing high-quality work.

Artisanal Crafts:
Artisanal crafts involve creating handmade and unique products, such as ceramics, jewellery, textiles, and woodwork. Artisans in this sector often sell their products at craft fairs, markets, and online platforms. They may also work with retailers to sell their products.

To succeed in the artisanal crafts sector, artisans must have strong craft skills and the ability to create unique and high-quality products that appeal to customers. They must also have good marketing skills to promote their products and build relationships with retailers.

Digital Art: The digital art sector involves creating art using digital tools and technologies, such as digital painting, graphic design, and animation. Digital artists often work in design firms, animation studios, and video game companies. They may also sell their work online or at art fairs. To succeed in the digital art sector, artists must have strong digital skills and knowledge of various digital tools and software. They must also be able to keep up with the latest trends in technology and design.

Conclusion:
Understanding your art business niche is critical to the success of your business. By identifying your niche, you can develop a business plan that caters to the specific needs of your target audience. This includes developing a brand identity, marketing strategies, and a sustainable business model. Regardless of your niche, it is essential to have strong technical skills, creative talent, and business acumen. These skills will help you succeed in the art industry and create a successful and fulfilling career. By following the tips outlined above and continuing to develop your skills, you can thrive in your art business and achieve your goals.

Your niche as a musician:

The music industry is diverse, and it can be challenging to navigate for those who are new to it. As with any business, identifying and understanding your niche is essential to creating a sustainable music career. Your niche is the specific area of the music industry that you specialize in or focus on. By understanding your niche, you can develop a business plan that caters to your target audience, build your brand identity, and create a sustainable business model.

Live Performance:
The live performance sector involves performing music live in front of an audience. This sector includes solo performances, bands, orchestras, and other musical ensembles. Artists in this sector usually earn money from ticket sales, merchandise sales, and performance fees.
To succeed in the live performance sector, artists must have excellent musical skills, a charismatic stage presence, and the ability to engage with the audience. They must also have strong marketing skills to promote their performances and build a loyal fan base.

Recording Artist:
The recording artist sector involves creating and recording music in a studio and releasing it as an album, single, or EP. Recording artists can earn money from streaming royalties, album sales, and merchandise sales. They may also perform live to promote their releases. To succeed in the recording artist sector, artists must have excellent musical skills, a unique sound and style, and the ability to connect with their audience. They must also have strong marketing skills to promote their releases and build a loyal fan base.

Music Production:
The music production sector involves producing music for other artists or for various media, such as film, television, and video games.
Music producers are responsible for creating the sound and arranging the music. They can earn money from production fees and royalties. To succeed in the music production sector, producers must have excellent technical skills, a creative vision, and the ability to work well with artists and clients. They

must also have strong marketing skills to promote their services and build a client base.

Music Education:

The music education sector involves teaching music to students of all ages. This sector includes music schools, universities, and community centres that offer music programs. Music educators may also work independently and offer private lessons or workshops. To succeed in the music education sector, educators must have excellent musical skills, a strong knowledge of music theory, and the ability to communicate effectively with students. They must also have strong marketing skills to promote their services and build a student base.

Music Management:

The music management sector involves managing the careers of musicians and other music industry professionals. Music managers are responsible for booking gigs, negotiating contracts, and managing finances. They can earn money from a percentage of the artist's earnings. To succeed in the music management sector, managers must have excellent organizational skills, a strong knowledge of the music industry, and the ability to negotiate effectively. They must also have strong marketing skills to promote their services and build a client base.

Conclusion:

Understanding your music business niche is crucial to the success of your music career. By identifying your niche, you can develop a business plan that caters to the specific needs of your target audience. This includes developing a brand identity, marketing strategies, and a sustainable business model. Regardless of your niche, it is essential to have strong musical skills, creative talent, and business acumen. These skills will help you succeed in the music industry and create a successful and fulfilling career.

By following the tips outlined above and continuing to develop your skills, you can thrive in your music business and achieve your goals.

Your niche as an Author

Introduction: The publishing industry can be overwhelming, and it can be challenging to navigate for those who are new to it. As with any business, identifying and understanding your niche is essential to creating a sustainable author career.

Your niche is the specific area of the publishing industry that you specialize in or focus on. By understanding your niche, you can develop a business plan that caters to your target audience, build your brand identity, and create a sustainable business model.

Genre Fiction:

Genre fiction involves writing books in specific genres such as romance, science fiction, fantasy, mystery, and thriller. Authors in this niche usually earn money from book sales and royalty payments. To succeed in the genre fiction sector, authors must have excellent writing skills, a unique voice, and the ability to connect with their target audience. They must also have strong marketing skills to promote their books and build a loyal fan base.

Nonfiction:

The nonfiction sector involves writing books on a particular subject such as self-help, memoir, biography, and history. Authors in this niche usually earn money from book sales and royalty payments. To succeed in the nonfiction sector, authors must have excellent writing skills, a strong knowledge of their subject, and the ability to connect with their target audience. They must also have strong marketing skills to promote their books and build a loyal fan base.

Children's Books:

The children's book sector involves writing books for young readers such as picture books, chapter books, and middle-grade books. Authors in this niche usually earn money from book sales and royalty payments.

To succeed in the children's book sector, authors must have excellent writing skills, a strong understanding of child development, and the ability to connect with their young audience.

They must also have strong marketing skills to promote their books and build a loyal fan base.

Academic and Scholarly Books:

The academic and scholarly book sector involves writing books on specific academic topics for university presses and scholarly publishers.
Authors in this niche usually earn money from book sales, royalty payments, and academic positions. To succeed in the academic and scholarly book sector, authors must have excellent research skills, a strong understanding of academic writing, and the ability to connect with their target audience. They must also have strong marketing skills to promote their books and build a loyal fan base.

Self-Publishing:
The self-publishing sector involves publishing books independently using online platforms such as Amazon Kindle Direct Publishing, IngramSpark, and Draft2Digital. Authors in this niche usually earn money from book sales and royalty payments. To succeed in the self-publishing sector, authors must have excellent writing skills, a strong understanding of self-publishing, and the ability to connect with their target audience. They must also have strong marketing skills to promote their books and build a loyal fan base.

Conclusion:
Understanding your author business niche is crucial to the success of your writing career. By identifying your niche, you can develop a business plan that caters to the specific needs of your target audience. This includes developing a brand identity, marketing strategies, and a sustainable business model. Regardless of your niche, it is essential to have strong writing skills, creative talent, and business acumen.
These skills will help you succeed in the publishing industry and create a successful and fulfilling career.
By following the tips outlined above and continuing to develop your skills, you can thrive in your author business and achieve your goals.

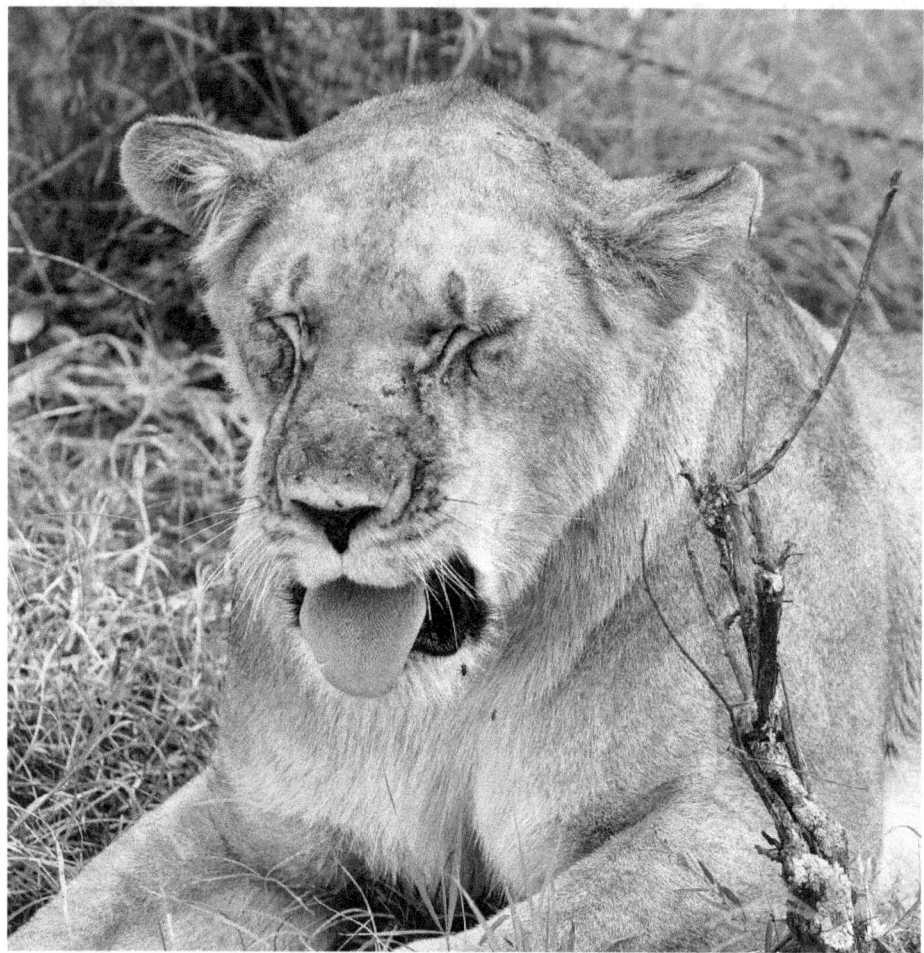

In business, there are many things which you will learn on your journey. Some which you will realise are already within you, and others which you need to learn and fast.

In this next section, I will begin teaching you some of the various assets that are a must in your business.

Chapter 3 The business side of things…

Websites:

In today's digital age, having a website is crucial for any business. A website can help you establish your online presence, showcase your products and services, and connect with your customers. For authors, speakers, and entrepreneurs, a website can be the key to building a successful online platform and growing your business. In this report, we will explore the process of setting up a website and discuss how you can best help your clients by following the advice of Donald Miller, author of the best-selling book "Building a StoryBrand."

Setting Up a website:
Choose a Domain Name:
A domain name is your website's address on the internet. When choosing a domain name, it is important to choose a name that is easy to remember and reflects your brand identity. Your domain name should also be relevant to your business and easy to spell.

Select a Web Hosting Service:
A web hosting service provides the server space where your website is stored and made accessible on the internet. When choosing a web hosting service, it is essential to select a provider that is reliable, secure, and affordable.

Develop a Website Design:
Your website design should reflect your brand identity and be visually appealing to your target audience. The design should be clean, easy to navigate, and optimized for both desktop and mobile devices. It should also include high-quality images, engaging copy, and clear calls-to-action.

Define Your Client's Story:
According to Donald Miller, the key to building a successful website is to define your client's story. This means identifying your client's pain points, their desires, and their motivations. By understanding your client's story, you can develop a website that speaks to their needs and engages them emotionally.

Clarify Your Message:
Once you have defined your client's story, it is essential to clarify their message. This involves identifying the unique value proposition that your client offers and communicating it clearly on their website. By clarifying your client's message, you can help them differentiate themselves from their competitors and stand out in their industry.

Make Your Website Easy to Navigate:
A key component of a successful website is its ease of navigation. By making your client's website easy to navigate, you can ensure that visitors can quickly find the information they are looking for. This involves organizing content into clear categories, using clear headings and subheadings, and using intuitive navigation menus. Remember what appears important to you may not to your potential clients. For example, if the house is flooded, your client could care less about when your business began, who founded it or where you went on your holiday last year. No! What they want to know is...
 1) Do you understand my problem
2) Can you fix my problem (And can you prove it)
3) What do I need to do for you to fix my problem?
The quicker you can provide the answers which your clients seek the better it is.
If you would like us to proof read your website and help you craft a masterful website then we do offer that service.
Details of this can be found on the last page.

Optimize Your Website for Conversions:
 Another crucial element of a successful website is its ability to convert visitors into customers.
To optimize your website for conversions, you should include clear calls-to-action, offer valuable content, and provide visitors with a clear path to purchase or contact your client.
Another way to optimize your website is by making use of SEO (Search Engine Optimization) this I shall cover in a later chapter (We also have a course which covers how to set up a creative website - in full). Details of this can be found at the end of this book.

Create Content for Your Website:

Your website content should be clear, concise, and informative. It should provide information about your products and services, showcase your expertise, and provide value to your target audience. Your content should also include keywords that will help your website rank higher in search engine results pages (SERPs).

Optimize Your Website for Search Engines:
Search engine optimization (SEO) is the process of optimizing your website to rank higher in search engine results pages (SERPs).
This involves incorporating keywords into your website content, optimizing your website design for mobile devices, and building high-quality backlinks to your website.

Helping Your Clients:
Define Your Client's Story.
According to Donald Miller, the key to building a successful website is to define your client's story. This means identifying your client's pain points, their desires, and their motivations. By understanding your client's story, you can develop a website that speaks to their needs and engages them emotionally.

Clarify Your Message:
 Once you have defined your client's story, it is essential to clarify your message. This involves identifying the unique value proposition that your offer your clients and communicating it clearly on your website. By clarifying your message, you can differentiate yourself from their competitors and stand out in your industry.

Make Your Website Easy to Navigate:
A key component of a successful website is its ease of navigation. By making your client's website easy to navigate, you can ensure that visitors can quickly find the information they are looking for. This involves organizing content into clear categories, using clear headings and subheadings, and using intuitive navigation menus.

Conclusion: Setting up a website can be a challenging task, but by following the tips outlined above and applying the advice of Donald Miller, you can create a successful online platform for your clients. By understanding your client's story, clarifying their message, and optimizing their website for conversions, you can help them achieve their goals and grow their business.

Marketing...

Marketing is essential for any business, but for creative businesses, it can be particularly challenging. Creative businesses are unique in that they rely on their creativity, skills, and innovation to differentiate themselves from their competitors and attract customers. In this section, we will explore the marketing framework developed by Donald Miller and how it can be applied to creative businesses.

Part 1: Introduction to the StoryBrand Marketing Framework: The StoryBrand marketing framework is a marketing strategy developed by Donald Miller, a best-selling author and marketing expert. The framework is based on the idea that every brand needs to tell a clear and compelling story that resonates with its target audience. The framework consists of seven elements, which are:

A character: The character is the hero of the story, and it is the customer who needs the product or service. A problem: The problem is the obstacle that the character is facing, and it is the reason why they need the product or service. A guide: The guide is the business or brand that offers the product or service, and it helps the character overcome the problem. A plan: The plan is the step-by-step process that the guide provides to help the character solve the problem.
A call to action: The call to action is the invitation to the customer to take action and purchase the product or service.

A failure:
The failure is what happens if the character does not take action and does not solve the problem.
A success: The success is what the character achieves after taking action and solving the problem.
Part 2:
Applying the StoryBrand Framework to Creative Businesses:
 Creative businesses can benefit from the StoryBrand framework by telling a clear and compelling story that resonates with their target audience. Here are some ways that creative businesses can apply the framework:

Identify the character:

Creative businesses should identify their target audience and understand their needs and wants. This will help them create a character that resonates with their target audience.

Identify the problem: Creative businesses should identify the problem that their target audience is facing and how their product or service can help solve it.

Position themselves as the guide:
Creative businesses should position themselves as the guide that can help their target audience overcome the problem. This can be achieved by highlighting their expertise, experience, and credentials.

Provide a clear plan: Creative businesses should provide a step-by-step process that their target audience can follow to solve the problem.

Include a call to action:
Creative businesses should include a clear and compelling call to action that encourages their target audience to act.

Highlight the consequences of not acting: Creative businesses should highlight the consequences of not taking action and not solving the problem.

Highlight the benefits of acting:
Creative businesses should highlight the benefits that their target audience can achieve by taking action and solving the problem.

Part 3: Examples of Creative Businesses That Have Successfully Applied the StoryBrand Framework:

There are many creative businesses that have successfully applied the StoryBrand framework to their marketing strategy.

Here are some examples: Apple: Apple's marketing strategy is based on the idea of simplicity. They position themselves as the guide that can help their customers overcome the problem of complex technology.

Their products are designed to be easy to use and understand, and their marketing materials are focused on the benefits of using their products.

Airbnb: Airbnb's marketing strategy is based on the idea of adventure and exploration. They position themselves as the guide that can help their customers overcome the problem of expensive and boring hotels. Their marketing materials focus on the benefits of staying in unique and interesting accommodations and exploring new places.

Nike: Nike's marketing strategy is based on the idea of empowerment. They position themselves as the guide that can help their customers overcome the problem of inactivity and help them achieve their fitness goals. Nike's marketing materials focus on the benefits of exercise and the sense of accomplishment that comes with achieving fitness goals. They use inspirational messaging and imagery to motivate their customers to take action and push themselves to new levels. Nike also utilizes storytelling to connect with their customers on a deeper level. For example, their "Dream Crazy" ad campaign featured stories of athletes who had overcome obstacles and achieved great success. These stories not only inspired customers but also helped them associate Nike with the idea of pushing oneself to achieve greatness.

In addition to their messaging, Nike also uses innovative technology to enhance their customers' fitness experience. They have developed products such as the Nike+ app and the Nike Fuelband, which help customers track their fitness progress and stay motivated. By combining their innovative products with their powerful messaging, Nike has been able to create a strong brand identity and a loyal customer base.

Part 4: Challenges Faced by Creative Businesses in Marketing Despite the benefits of the StoryBrand framework, creative businesses face unique challenges in marketing. One of the main challenges is that creativity can be subjective, and it can be difficult to communicate the value of creative work to customers. Creative businesses must find ways to communicate the value of their work in a way that resonates with their target audience. Another challenge is that creative businesses often operate in niche markets, which can make it difficult to reach a broader audience.

They must find ways to reach customers who appreciate their work and are willing to pay for it. Lastly, creative businesses often have limited resources, which can make it difficult to invest in marketing. They must find ways to be creative with their marketing strategies and make the most of their resources.

Part 5: Conclusion:
Marketing is essential for any business, and creative businesses are no exception. By applying the StoryBrand framework, creative businesses can create a clear and compelling story that resonates with their target audience. However, creative businesses face unique challenges in marketing and must find ways to communicate the value of their work and reach a broader audience. By being creative with their marketing strategies and leveraging

innovative technology, creative businesses can build a strong brand identity and achieve success in the marketplace.

Sales... Getting it right

Introduction...

  Sales are essential for any business, and creative businesses are no exception. However, selling creative products or services can be challenging, as creativity is often subjective, and customers may not fully understand the value of the work. In this essay, we will explore sales strategies for creative businesses based on the teachings of Victor Antonio, a sales expert, author, and speaker. We will examine how creative businesses can apply these strategies to increase their sales and achieve success in the marketplace.

Part 1: Understanding the Sales Process The sales process is the sequence of steps that a salesperson follows to persuade a potential customer to buy a product or service. The sales process typically involves several stages, including prospecting, qualifying, presenting, handling objections, closing the sale, and follow-up. In the prospecting stage, the salesperson identifies potential customers and gathers information about their needs and preferences. This information is used to qualify the leads and determine if they are a good fit for the product or service. Once the leads are qualified, the salesperson presents the product or service to the customer, highlighting its unique features and benefits. The salesperson must also address any objections or concerns that the customer may have. If the customer is interested in the product or service, the salesperson moves on to the closing stage, where they ask for the sale and handle any final objections.

Once the sale is closed, the salesperson follows up with the customer to ensure their satisfaction and potentially upsell or cross-sell additional products or services.

Part 2: Applying Sales Strategies to Creative Businesses Creative businesses can use several strategies to increase their sales and improve their success in the marketplace.

Some of the key strategies are outlined below: Know Your Customer To be successful in sales, creative businesses must understand their target customers' needs, preferences, and pain points. By knowing their customers, creative businesses can tailor their sales pitches to address their specific concerns and highlight the unique features and benefits of their products or services. Focus on the Benefits In selling creative products or services, it is crucial to focus on the benefits rather than the features.

Features are the technical aspects of the product or service, while benefits are the outcomes that the customer will experience. By emphasizing the benefits, creative businesses can show customers the value of their work and how it can meet their needs.

Tell a Compelling Story: Creative businesses can use storytelling to connect with their customers on a deeper level. By sharing the inspiration and motivation behind their work, creative businesses can create an emotional connection with their customers and help them understand the value of their work.

Build Relationships: In selling creative products or services, building relationships is essential. Creative businesses must work to build trust and rapport with their customers and show them that they are invested in their success. By building relationships, creative businesses can create loyal customers who will return for future work and refer others to their business. Embrace Technology: Technology can be a powerful tool for creative businesses to increase their sales. By leveraging technology, creative businesses can reach a broader audience, showcase their work, and streamline the sales process. Examples of technology that creative businesses can use include social media, email marketing, and online marketplaces.

Overcome Objections:
In selling creative products or services, customers may have objections or concerns.
It is essential for salespeople to address these objections and show customers how their product or service can meet their needs. By overcoming objections, creative businesses can build trust and confidence with their customers and increase their chances of making a sale.

Part 3: Sales Strategies for Creative Businesses Now that we have outlined some key strategies for creative businesses to improve their sales, let us examine some specific sales strategies that creative businesses can implement.

Network and Collaborate Networking and collaborating with other businesses and professionals in the industry can be an effective way for creative businesses to increase their sales. By forming partnerships and collaborations, creative businesses can expand their reach, access new customers, and learn from other industry experts. Networking events, industry conferences, and social media platforms can all be used to connect with other businesses and professionals in the industry.

Creative businesses can also reach out to complementary businesses to explore opportunities for collaboration, such as joint marketing efforts or cross-promotions.

Develop a Strong Brand Identity:
In the creative industry, a strong brand identity can be a powerful tool for increasing sales. By developing a unique and memorable brand identity, creative businesses can differentiate themselves from the competition and create a strong connection with their target audience. A strong brand identity includes elements such as a distinctive logo, consistent branding across all marketing materials, and a clear mission and vision statement. By developing a strong brand identity, creative businesses can build trust with their customers and increase their chances of making a sale. Use Testimonials and Case Studies Testimonials and case studies can be effective tools for building credibility and trust with potential customers.

By showcasing previous work and customer feedback, creative businesses can demonstrate their expertise and the value of their work. Testimonials can be collected from previous clients and displayed on the business's website or social media platforms. Case studies can be used to showcase the creative process and results of previous projects, highlighting the value that the business can provide to potential customers.

Leverage Content Marketing:
Content marketing is a marketing strategy that involves creating and sharing valuable content to attract and engage a target audience. In the creative industry, content marketing can be used to showcase a business's expertise, build brand awareness, and attract potential customers. Creative businesses can create content such as blog posts, videos, and social media posts that showcase their work and provide valuable information to potential customers.

By sharing this content, creative businesses can establish themselves as thought leaders in the industry and attract a loyal following of customers.

Offer Customization and Personalization:
Creative businesses can increase their sales by offering customization and personalization options to customers. By tailoring their products or services to the unique needs and preferences of each customer, creative businesses can demonstrate the value of their work and create a more personalized experience for the customer. Customization options can include elements such as color, size, or design. Personalization options can include features such as customized messaging or personalized packaging. By offering customization and personalization options, creative businesses can differentiate themselves from the competition and increase their chances of making a sale.

Provide Exceptional Customer Service:
Providing exceptional customer service is essential for any business, and creative businesses are no exception.
By providing excellent customer service, creative businesses can build trust and loyalty with their customers and increase their chances of making a sale. Exceptional customer service includes elements such as timely responses to inquiries and questions, clear communication throughout the sales process, and a focus on customer satisfaction. By prioritizing the customer's needs and providing a positive experience, creative businesses can create loyal customers who will return for future work and refer others to the business.

Conclusion:
Sales are essential for any business, and creative businesses are no exception. By understanding the sales process and implementing effective sales strategies, creative businesses can increase their sales and achieve success in the marketplace. Networking and collaborating with other businesses, developing a strong brand identity, using testimonials and case studies, leveraging content marketing, offering customization and personalization, and providing exceptional customer service are all effective strategies that creative businesses can use to improve their sales. By implementing these strategies and focusing on the unique value of their work, creative businesses can differentiate themselves from the competition and build a loyal customer base. With a strong sales strategy in place, creative businesses can achieve success and thrive in the ever-evolving creative industry.

Pricing...

This is the one thing which trips up everybody I have ever worked with. Reader, pay special attention in this section. Pricing is a critical aspect of any business, and creative businesses are no exception. Setting the right price for creative products and services can be a challenge, as they are often subjective and difficult to quantify. However, by understanding the pricing strategies and factors that impact pricing in the creative industry, creative businesses can set the right price for their work and achieve success in the marketplace. This article will explore the various pricing strategies that creative businesses can use, the factors that impact pricing in the creative industry, and how creative businesses can effectively price their products and services.

Strategies for Creative Businesses:
Cost-Plus Pricing Cost-plus pricing is a straightforward pricing strategy that involves adding a markup to the cost of producing a product or providing a service. This markup is typically a percentage of the cost and is intended to cover overhead expenses and provide a profit. Cost-plus pricing can be an effective strategy for creative businesses that have a good understanding of their costs and overhead expenses.

However, it may not always be the most appropriate pricing strategy for creative businesses, as it does not take into account the perceived value of the product or service. Value-Based Pricing Value-based pricing is a pricing strategy that focuses on the perceived value of the product or service to the customer. This strategy involves setting a price that reflects the value that the product or service provides to the customer, rather than simply adding a markup to the cost of production. Value-based pricing can be an effective strategy for creative businesses, as it considers the unique value that their work provides to customers.

By understanding the perceived value of their work, creative businesses can set a price that accurately reflects this value and increase their chances of making a sale. Hourly or Daily Rates Hourly or daily rates are a common pricing strategy for creative businesses that offer services such as design, photography, or writing. This strategy involves setting a fixed hourly or daily rate for the work performed, which is charged to the customer. Hourly or daily rates can be an effective pricing strategy for creative businesses that have a good understanding of the time required to complete a project. However, it may not always be the most appropriate pricing strategy, as it does not consider the value that the work provides to the customer. Package Pricing Package pricing is a pricing strategy that involves offering a bundled package of products or services at a set price.

Creative businesses must understand the perceived value of their work and set a price that accurately reflects this value. By focusing on the perceived value, creative businesses can differentiate themselves from their competitors and increase their chances of making a sale. Production Costs Production costs are the costs associated with producing a product or providing a service. These costs can include materials, labor, and overhead expenses.

Creative businesses must have a good understanding of their production costs to ensure that they are pricing their products and services effectively. By accurately calculating production costs, creative businesses can determine the minimum price that they need to charge to cover their costs and generate a profit. It is important to note that production costs can vary significantly depending on the nature of the product or service. For example, a digital product may have relatively low production costs, as it does not require physical materials or shipping. On the other hand, a handmade product may have higher production costs, as it requires more time and materials to produce.

Target Market:
The target market is the group of customers that a creative business is aiming to reach. The target market can impact pricing, as different groups of customers may have different price sensitivities and perceptions of value. For example, luxury products and services may be priced higher to appeal to customers who value exclusivity and quality, while more affordable products and services may be priced lower to appeal to price-sensitive customers. Brand Image Brand image is the perception that customers have of a business and its products or services. The brand image can impact pricing, as customers may be willing to pay more for products or services that are associated with a high-quality or prestigious brand.

This strategy can be effective for creative businesses that offer a range of products or services, as it simplifies the pricing process for customers and can increase the perceived value of the offer. Package pricing can also be used to incentivize customers to purchase multiple products or services, as the bundled price is often lower than the total cost of purchasing each product or service separately.

Factors That Impact Pricing in the Creative Industry... Competition: Competition is a key factor that impacts pricing in the creative industry. Creative businesses must be aware of their competitors' pricing and position themselves accordingly to remain competitive. However, it is essential to remember that price should not be the only factor that differentiates a business from its competitors. Perceived Value Perceived value is the value that a product or service provides to the customer, as perceived by the customer. In the creative industry, perceived value can be challenging to quantify, as creative products and services are often subjective and difficult to measure.

Determine Your Brand Image: Your brand image can impact your pricing strategy, as customers may be willing to pay more for products or services that are associated with a high-quality or prestigious brand. To determine your brand image, consider the unique qualities that your business and products or services offer. By building a strong brand and positioning yourself as a high-quality and prestigious business, you can justify a higher price point and increase the perceived value of your products and services.

Conclusion:
   Pricing is a critical aspect of any creative business and can have a significant impact on the success of the business. It is important for creative businesses to understand the various factors that can impact pricing, such as production costs, competition, target market, perceived value, and brand image. To determine the optimal pricing strategy, creative businesses must carefully consider these factors and find a balance between generating profit and providing value to their customers. By accurately calculating production costs, researching the competition, understanding their target market, focusing on perceived value, and building a strong brand image, creative businesses can develop a pricing strategy that supports their long-term success. It is also important for creative businesses to regularly review and adjust their pricing strategy as market conditions and business needs change.

Chapter 4 Website's part II... SEO

Search engine optimization (SEO) has become a crucial aspect of digital marketing for businesses in almost every industry. For creative businesses, such as artists, designers, and musicians, understanding SEO is especially important as it can significantly impact their online visibility and reach. In this essay, we will explore the importance of understanding SEO for creative businesses and how it can help them to succeed in the modern digital landscape.

What is SEO? SEO is the practice of optimizing a website and its content to rank higher in search engine results pages (SERPs). The goal of SEO is to increase organic traffic to a website by improving its visibility and relevance to search engines like Google. By improving their search engine rankings, businesses can attract more visitors to their website, generate more leads, and ultimately increase sales and revenue.

Importance of SEO for Creative Businesses Increased Online Visibility For creative businesses, online visibility is essential for reaching a wider audience and gaining recognition. By optimizing their website and content for search engines, creative businesses can increase their online visibility, which can help to attract more visitors to their website and increase brand awareness. This increased online visibility can also help creative businesses to establish themselves as thought leaders and experts in their field.

Cost-effective Marketing SEO is a cost-effective marketing strategy, especially when compared to traditional advertising methods. By optimizing their website and content for search engines, creative businesses can attract more organic traffic to their website without having to pay for expensive advertising. This can help them to save on marketing costs and invest more resources in other areas of their business. Targeted Traffic One of the biggest advantages of SEO is that it can help to attract targeted traffic to a website.

This means that the people who visit a creative business's website are more likely to be interested in their products or services. This can result in higher conversion rates and a better return on investment for marketing efforts. Competitive Advantage In a highly competitive industry, SEO can provide creative businesses with a competitive advantage by helping them to stand out in search engine results pages. By optimizing their website and content for search engines, creative businesses can outrank their competitors and attract more visitors to their website. This can help them to establish themselves as leaders in their field and gain an edge over their competitors. Improved User Experience SEO is not just about optimizing a website for search engines, but also for the user experience.

By improving the user experience of their website, creative businesses can help to keep visitors engaged and increase the chances of conversion. A well-optimized website can also help to reduce bounce rates and increase the time spent on a website, which can positively impact search engine rankings.

Understanding SEO for Creative Businesses Keyword Research Keyword research is a critical aspect of SEO and involves identifying the keywords and phrases that people use to search for products or services related to a creative business. By conducting keyword research, creative businesses can identify the most relevant and high-volume keywords in their industry and optimize their website and content around those keywords.

On-Page Optimization On-page optimization involves optimizing the content on a website for search engines. This includes optimizing titles, headings, meta descriptions, and content for keywords and making sure that the website is easy to navigate and user-friendly. Off-Page Optimization Off-page optimization involves optimizing a website's external factors, such as backlinks and social media presence.

By building high-quality backlinks and engaging with their audience on social media, creative businesses can improve their online reputation and increase their visibility in search engine results pages. Mobile Optimization With the rise of mobile devices, mobile optimization has become a crucial aspect of SEO.

Creative businesses must ensure that their website is mobile-friendly and responsive, as this can impact their search engine rankings and user experience. Analytics and Monitoring Analytics and monitoring are crucial aspects of understanding the effectiveness of an SEO strategy.

Creative businesses must regularly monitor their website's traffic and engagement metrics to understand which strategies are working and which ones need improvement. This includes tracking keyword rankings, traffic sources, bounce rates, and conversion rates.

By monitoring their website's analytics, creative businesses can make data-driven decisions and adjust their SEO strategy accordingly to improve their online visibility and attract more organic traffic to their website. Stay Up-to-Date with Algorithm Updates Search engine algorithms are constantly changing, and creative businesses must stay up-to-date with these changes to ensure that their SEO strategy is effective.

Understanding the latest algorithm updates and trends can help creative businesses to adapt their SEO strategy and stay ahead of the competition. Conclusion In conclusion, understanding SEO is essential for the success of creative businesses in the modern digital landscape. By optimizing their website and content for search engines, creative businesses can increase their online visibility, attract more targeted traffic, and gain a competitive advantage over their competitors.

Creative businesses must understand the importance of keyword research, on-page and off-page optimization, mobile optimization, analytics and monitoring, and staying up-to-date with algorithm updates to create an effective SEO strategy that can help them achieve their marketing goals. With a well-executed SEO strategy, creative businesses can attract more organic traffic to their website, increase their brand awareness, and generate more leads and sales.

So how do you do it?

Search engine optimization (SEO) is an essential process that can help creative businesses to improve their online visibility, attract more targeted traffic, and generate more leads and sales. However, implementing an effective SEO strategy for creative websites can be challenging due to the unique nature of creative content. In this article, we will discuss some tips on how to do SEO on creative websites. Conduct Keyword Research Keyword research is a critical step in any SEO strategy, and it is particularly important for creative websites. Creative businesses must understand the language and search terms that their target audience is using to find content relevant to their niche. Conducting keyword research can help creative businesses to identify the keywords and phrases that their target audience is using to search for creative content, and optimize their website and content accordingly.

Tools such as Google Keyword Planner, SEMrush, and Ahrefs can help creative businesses to conduct keyword research, identify search volume and competition levels for specific keywords, and generate keyword ideas. Optimize On-Page Elements On-page optimization is the process of optimizing the content and structure of a website to improve its visibility in search engine rankings.

Build High-Quality Backlinks:

Backlinks are a crucial aspect of SEO, and they can help creative businesses to improve their website's domain authority, traffic, and search engine rankings. Creative businesses must build high-quality backlinks from relevant and authoritative websites to demonstrate the value and relevance of their content to search engines. Creative businesses can build high-quality backlinks by creating engaging and shareable content, collaborating with other creatives and businesses in their niche, and using social media to promote their content and website. Optimize for Mobile Devices Mobile optimization is an essential aspect of SEO for creative websites. With an increasing number of internet users accessing the internet through mobile devices, creative businesses must ensure that their website is optimized for mobile devices to provide a positive user experience.

Creative businesses must ensure that their website is mobile-friendly, with fast load times and a responsive design that adjusts to different screen sizes. Mobile optimization can help to improve the user experience, reduce bounce rates, and increase the time spent on the website, which can all contribute to higher search engine rankings. Conclusion In conclusion, SEO is a critical process for creative businesses to improve their online visibility and attract more targeted traffic to their website. By following the tips outlined in this article, creative businesses can conduct effective keyword research, optimize on-page elements, create high-quality and engaging content, build high-quality backlinks, and optimize their website for mobile devices to create an effective SEO strategy for their creative website.

Optimize On-Page Elements On-page optimization is the process of optimizing the content and structure of a website to improve its visibility in search engine rankings. Creative businesses must optimize on-page elements such as meta titles and descriptions, headers, image alt tags, and internal linking to ensure that search engines can crawl and index their website effectively. When optimizing on-page elements for creative websites, it is essential to use descriptive and relevant keywords in the meta titles and descriptions, headers, and image alt tags.

 Creative businesses can also use internal linking to create a logical structure for their website and help search engines to understand the hierarchy and relevance of their content. Create High-Quality, Unique, and Engaging Content Creative businesses must create high-quality, unique, and engaging content to attract and retain their target audience.

Search engines prioritize high-quality and engaging content in their rankings, and creative businesses must ensure that their content meets these standards. When creating content for creative websites, it is important to write for humans first, and search engines second. Creative businesses must use relevant keywords and phrases in their content to help search engines understand the topic and relevance of their content. However, they must also ensure that the content is well-written, informative, and engaging for their target audience.

However, it is important to remember that SEO is an ongoing process that requires regular monitoring, testing, and adjustment to ensure that the strategy is effective. Creative businesses must also ensure that their SEO strategy aligns with their overall business goals, branding, and target audience. By understanding the unique characteristics of their creative business and audience, creative businesses can create an SEO strategy that is tailored to their specific needs and goals. In addition to SEO, creative businesses should also consider implementing other digital marketing strategies, such as social media marketing, email marketing, and paid advertising, to complement their SEO efforts and drive even more traffic and sales to their website.
Overall, SEO is a crucial aspect of digital marketing for creative businesses, and by following the tips outlined in this article, creative businesses can create an effective SEO strategy that helps them to achieve their business goals and grow their creative business.

Chapter 5 Making money!

As an artist, you may have a passion for creating art, but you may also need to make a living from it. Fortunately, there are many ways to monetize your art, and with the right strategy, you can build a successful and sustainable career. Here are some ways to make money with your art:

Sell your art:
The most obvious way to make money with your art is to sell it. You can sell your art in a variety of ways, including online marketplaces, art fairs, galleries, and exhibitions. When selling your art, it's important to price it correctly, market it effectively, and offer a seamless buying experience for your customers. Offer art lessons or workshops: You can also monetize your art by teaching others how to create it. You can offer art lessons or workshops in person or online, and charge a fee for your time and expertise. This can be a great way to supplement your income and build your reputation as an artist.

Sell merchandise:
You can create merchandise featuring your art, such as prints, t-shirts, mugs, and phone cases, and sell them online or in-person. This allows you to reach a wider audience and generate more revenue from your art. License your art: You can license your art to companies, organizations, or individuals who want to use it for commercial purposes. This can include anything from book covers to product packaging, and can be a lucrative way to make money with your art.

Grants and awards:
Many organizations offer grants and awards to support artists and their work. These can be a great way to receive financial support and gain recognition for your art. Art residency programs: Art residency programs offer artists the opportunity to create new work in a supportive environment. Many art residencies provide financial support, workspace, and other resources to help artists focus on their creative work.

Crowdfunding:
Crowdfunding is a popular way to raise funds for creative projects. You can use crowdfunding platforms to raise money for your art, such as to fund a new exhibition or art project. Crowdfunding can be a great way to get financial support from your audience while building a community around your work. Commissions: You can also make money by accepting commissions for custom art pieces. This allows you to create art that is tailored to a specific customer's needs and preferences, and you can charge a premium price for your services.

Art auctions:
You can also sell your art through auctions, either in person or online. Auctions can be a great way to reach a wider audience and generate higher prices for your art. Art licensing agencies: Art licensing agencies act as intermediaries between artists and companies that want to license their art. These agencies can help you monetize your art by connecting you with potential clients and managing the licensing process.

In conclusion, there are many ways to monetize your art, and it's important to find the right strategy that works for you. Whether you sell your art, teach others, create merchandise, or license your work, with the right approach and persistence, you can build a successful and sustainable career as an artist.

Tips for making money as a musician.

Making money with your music can be challenging, but there are many ways to monetize your music and build a sustainable career as a musician. Here are some ways to make money with your music:

Sell your music:
 The most obvious way to make money with your music is to sell it. You can sell your music on digital music platforms such as iTunes, Amazon Music, and Google Play, or you can sell physical copies of your music, such as CDs and vinyl records.

Perform live: Live performances can be a significant source of income for musicians. You can perform at concerts, festivals, and other events, and charge a fee for your performance. You can also sell merchandise at your live shows, such as t-shirts, posters, and other items featuring your music.
 Licensing: You can license your music to film, TV, and other media projects. This can include anything from commercials to movie soundtracks. You can work with music licensing agencies or directly with producers and directors to get your music licensed.

Royalties: You can earn royalties from your music through various sources, such as streaming services like Spotify, Apple Music, and Pandora. You can also earn royalties from radio airplay, live performances, and other sources. Crowdfunding: Crowdfunding is a popular way to raise funds for creative projects. You can use crowdfunding platforms to raise money for your music, such as to fund a new album or music video.

Crowdfunding can be a great way to get financial support from your fans while building a community around your music. Merchandise: You can create merchandise featuring your music, such as t-shirts, hats, and other items, and sell them online or at your live shows. This can be a great way to generate additional revenue and promote your music. Teaching: You can also make money by teaching others how to play music. You can offer music lessons in person or online, and charge a fee for your time and expertise.

Song writing:
You can also make money by writing songs for other artists or licensing your songs to other musicians. This can be a great way to earn income while

promoting your own music. Fan clubs: You can create a fan club for your music and offer exclusive content, merchandise, and other perks to your most dedicated fans.

This can be a great way to build a community around your music and generate additional income. In conclusion, there are many ways to make money with your music, and it's important to find the right strategy that works for you. Whether you sell your music, perform live, license your music, or create merchandise, with the right approach and persistence, you can build a successful and sustainable career as a musician.

Tips for making money as an Author.

Making money with your writing can be challenging, but there are many ways to monetize your work and build a sustainable career as an author. Here are some ways to make money with your writing:

Sell your books:
The most obvious way to make money with your writing is to sell your books. You can publish your books through traditional publishing houses, self-publishing platforms, or hybrid publishing companies. You can sell your books on online platforms such as Amazon, Barnes & Noble, and Kobo, or you can sell them in brick-and-mortar bookstores.

Speaking engagements:
You can also make money by speaking at events and conferences. You can offer keynote speeches, workshops, and other presentations based on your area of expertise. This can be a great way to promote your books and build your brand. Freelance writing: You can also make money by writing for magazines, newspapers, and other publications. You can pitch article ideas to editors, or you can write for content mills and other online platforms.

Freelance writing can be a great way to supplement your income and build your writing portfolio. Ghost-writing: You can also make money by ghost-writing for other authors or professionals. You can write books, articles, and other content for clients, and charge a fee for your work. Writing coaching: You can also make money by offering writing coaching services.

You can help other writers improve their craft, provide feedback on their work, and help them navigate the publishing process. Writing coaching can be a great way to build your reputation as an expert in your field. Online courses: You can also make money by creating and selling online courses related to writing. You can offer courses on topics such as writing craft, self-publishing, and book marketing. Online courses can be a great way to reach a wider audience and build your reputation as an expert in your field.

Patreon and crowdfunding:
You can also make money by using platforms like Patreon and crowdfunding to fund your writing projects. These platforms allow your fans to support your work by contributing to your project on a monthly or one-time basis. Affiliate

marketing: You can also make money by promoting other writers' books and products through affiliate marketing.

You can earn a commission on sales made through your affiliate links. Writing contests and grants: You can also make money by participating in writing contests and applying for grants. Many organizations offer grants and prizes to support writers and their work. In conclusion, there are many ways to make money with your writing, and it's important to find the right strategy that works for you. Whether you sell your books, offer speaking engagements, freelance write, or create online courses, with the right approach and persistence, you can build a successful and sustainable career as an author.

Affiliate marketing: You can also make money by promoting other writers' books and products through affiliate marketing. You can earn a commission on sales made through your affiliate links. Writing contests and grants: You can also make money by participating in writing contests and applying for grants. Many organizations offer grants and prizes to support writers and their work. In conclusion, there are many ways to make money with your writing, and it's important to find the right strategy that works for you. Whether you sell your books, offer speaking engagements, freelance write, or create online courses, with the right approach and persistence, you can build a successful and sustainable career as an author.

Chapter 6 - social media and its uses...

Social media has become an integral part of our daily lives, and it has revolutionized the way we connect, communicate, and consume content. For creative minds, social media offers a powerful platform to showcase their work, build their brand, and connect with others in their industry. In this essay, we will explore the importance of social media for creative minds and how it can be used to maximize their potential. Firstly, social media provides creative minds with a global audience. Unlike traditional methods of promoting their work, social media allows creatives to reach a broad and diverse audience with just a few clicks. With over 3.78 billion active users, social media platforms such as Instagram, Twitter, Facebook, and YouTube have become the go-to destination for artists, writers, designers, and other creative professionals to showcase their work and attract new fans and followers.

Secondly, social media is a powerful tool for brand building. By consistently posting their work, creatives can create a brand identity and a recognizable visual style that can help them stand out from the competition. Social media platforms offer various features such as hashtags, geotags, and stories to help creatives build their brand and create a loyal following. By leveraging these features, creatives can create a strong online presence and build a personal brand that resonates with their target audience.

Thirdly, social media provides creatives with opportunities for collaboration and networking. Through social media, creatives can connect with other artists, designers, and professionals in their industry, and collaborate on projects, share ideas and techniques.
 This can lead to new opportunities, such as exhibitions, publications, and commissions, which can help creatives grow their career and reach new audiences. Fourthly, social media offers valuable feedback and insights.

Through social media analytics, creatives can gather data on their audience, such as their demographics, interests, and preferences. This information can help creatives understand their target audience better and tailor their content to meet their needs. Additionally, social media offers a space for creatives to receive feedback and constructive criticism from their audience, which can help them improve their work and grow as artists.

Finally, social media offers a space for creatives to stay up to date with the latest trends and news in their industry. By following other creatives and industry experts, creatives can stay informed on the latest techniques, tools, and trends. This can help them improve their skills, stay ahead of the competition, and adapt to changes in the industry.

In conclusion, social media has become a vital tool for creative minds. From reaching a global audience to building a personal brand, social media offers creatives the opportunity to showcase their work and build a loyal following. Additionally, social media offers opportunities for collaboration, feedback, and networking, which can help creatives grow their career and reach new heights. Therefore, it is essential for creative minds to leverage the power of social media and use it to maximize their potential.

Facebook

Facebook is one of the world's largest social media platforms, with over 2.8 billion monthly active users. It has become a crucial tool for creative businesses, providing a space to showcase their work, build their brand, and connect with their target audience. In this essay, we will explore the importance of Facebook for creative businesses and how it can be used to maximize their potential.

Firstly, Facebook provides creative businesses with a global audience. With a vast user base, Facebook offers businesses the opportunity to reach a broad and diverse audience, regardless of their location. This can be especially valuable for businesses that are just starting or those looking to expand their reach. Through Facebook's powerful targeting tools, businesses can reach a specific audience based on factors such as age, location, interests, and behaviours. This can help businesses to target their ideal customers and maximize their marketing efforts.

Secondly, Facebook is a powerful tool for brand building. By consistently posting their work, businesses can create a recognizable brand identity and a loyal following. Facebook offers various features, such as pages, groups, and ads, to help businesses build their brand and engage with their audience. Pages allow businesses to create a professional online presence that includes their logo, description, and contact information. Groups provide a space for businesses to connect with their audience, share content, and build a community around their brand. Ads allow businesses to target specific audiences and drive traffic to their website or products.

Thirdly, Facebook provides creative businesses with opportunities for collaboration and networking. Through Facebook, businesses can connect with other businesses, industry experts, and potential customers. This can lead to new opportunities, such as partnerships, collaborations, and events, which can help businesses grow their brand and reach new audiences. Additionally, Facebook provides a space for businesses to receive feedback and constructive criticism from their audience, which can help them improve their work and grow as businesses.

Fourthly, Facebook offers valuable insights and analytics. Through Facebook's Page Insights, businesses can gather data on their audience, such as their demographics, interests, and behaviours. This information can help businesses understand their target audience better and tailor their content to meet their needs. Additionally, Facebook offers a space for businesses to track the performance of their posts, ads, and campaigns. This can help businesses measure their success and make informed decisions about their marketing efforts.

Fifthly, Facebook offers a space for businesses to stay up to date with the latest trends and news in their industry. By following other businesses and industry experts, businesses can stay informed on the latest techniques, tools, and trends. This can help them improve their skills, stay ahead of the competition, and adapt to changes in the industry.

Lastly, Facebook is an affordable and cost-effective marketing tool. Unlike traditional marketing methods, such as print ads or television commercials, Facebook offers businesses the opportunity to reach a large audience at a low cost. Businesses can choose from a variety of advertising options, including boosted posts, page likes, and website clicks, and set their budget and target audience. This can be especially valuable for small businesses or those with a limited marketing budget.

In conclusion, Facebook has become a crucial tool for creative businesses. From reaching a global audience to building a loyal following, Facebook offers businesses the opportunity to showcase their work and build their brand. Additionally, Facebook provides opportunities for collaboration, networking, and valuable insights and analytics. Therefore, it is essential for creative businesses to leverage the power of Facebook and use it to maximize their potential.

Here are some tips for using Facebook for creative businesses:
Create a professional and engaging Facebook page:
The first step is to create a Facebook page that is professional and engaging. Use a high-quality profile picture and cover photo that represents your brand. Ensure that your page has complete information about your business, such as your description, contact information, and website link.

Post consistently: Posting regularly is important to keep your audience engaged and interested in your brand. Create a content calendar and plan out your posts in advance. Share a mix of content, including your work, behind-the-scenes glimpses, and relevant industry news.

Engage with your audience: Respond to comments and messages promptly and engage with your audience. This will help you build a loyal following and create a community around your brand. Encourage feedback and respond to constructive criticism with an open mind.

Use Facebook groups: Join relevant Facebook groups related to your industry and participate in conversations.
Share your work and engage with the group members. Additionally, consider creating your own Facebook group to build a community around your brand and connect with your audience.

 Leverage Facebook Ads: Facebook Ads can be a powerful tool to reach your target audience and promote your business.
Use Facebook's targeting tools to create ads that target a specific audience based on factors such as age, location, interests, and behaviours. Set a budget and monitor the performance of your ads.

Use Facebook Live: Facebook Live is a powerful tool to connect with your audience in real-time. Use it to showcase your work, provide tutorials, or answer questions from your audience.

This will help you build a personal connection with your audience and create a loyal following.

Use Facebook Insights: Facebook Insights provides valuable data on your audience, including their demographics, interests, and behaviours. Use this data to understand your audience better and tailor your content to meet their needs. Additionally, use Facebook Insights to track the performance of your posts, ads, and campaigns. By following these tips, creative businesses can leverage the power of Facebook to build their brand, connect with their audience, and grow their business.

Instagram

Instagram has become an essential platform for creative businesses, providing a visual and engaging way to showcase their work and connect with potential customers. With over a billion active users, Instagram has become an important marketing tool for businesses of all sizes. In this article, we will explore the importance of Instagram for creative businesses and share some tips for maximizing your impact on the platform. Why is Instagram Important for Creative Businesses?

Visual platform: Instagram is a visual platform, making it the perfect platform for creative businesses to showcase their work. Through high-quality images and videos, businesses can create a strong visual identity, showcase their products, and engage with their audience.

Reach a broader audience: Instagram allows businesses to reach a broader audience beyond their physical location. Through the use of hashtags and location tagging, businesses can connect with potential customers from all over the world. Engage with your audience: Instagram provides a direct and personal way to engage with your audience. By responding to comments, direct messages, and engaging with your audience, you can build relationships and create a loyal following.

Build brand identity: Instagram provides a platform to showcase your brand identity and create a cohesive and visually appealing brand. By curating your feed and sharing consistent content, you can create a strong brand identity that resonates with your audience.

Tips for Maximizing Your Impact on Instagram:

Create a visually appealing feed: The first step to maximizing your impact on Instagram is to create a visually appealing feed. Choose a consistent color palette, use high-quality images and videos, and curate your content to create a cohesive brand identity.

Use Instagram Stories: Instagram Stories are a great way to engage with your audience and share behind-the-scenes content. Use features such as polls, questions, and quizzes to encourage engagement and build a relationship with your audience.

Use hashtags: Hashtags are a powerful tool to increase the reach of your posts and connect with your target audience. Use relevant hashtags in your posts and stories to increase your visibility and reach new followers.

Engage with your audience: Engage with your audience by responding to comments, direct messages, and sharing user-generated content. By building a relationship with your audience, you can create a loyal following and increase brand awareness.

Use Instagram Shopping: Instagram Shopping is a powerful tool for creative businesses to sell their products directly on the platform. By tagging products in your posts and stories, customers can easily purchase products directly from your feed.

Collaborate with influencers: Influencer marketing is a powerful way to reach a broader audience and build brand awareness. Partner with influencers in your industry to promote your products and increase your reach.

Use Instagram Ads: Instagram Ads are a powerful tool to reach a broader audience and promote your business. Use targeting features such as demographics, interests, and behaviours to create ads that reach your target audience.

In conclusion, Instagram is an essential platform for creative businesses to showcase their work, engage with their audience, and build their brand. By following the tips mentioned above, businesses can maximize their impact on the platform and grow their business.

Tik Tok

TikTok is a social media platform that has taken the world by storm, particularly among younger audiences. With its short-form video format, creative businesses have found a new way to showcase their products and engage with their audience. In this article, we will explore the importance of TikTok for creative businesses and share some tips for maximizing your impact on the platform.

Why is TikTok Important for Creative Businesses?
Reach a younger audience: TikTok has become particularly popular among younger audiences, making it an excellent platform for businesses that target a younger demographic. With over 1 billion active users, TikTok provides a huge potential audience for businesses.

Showcasing products in a creative way:
TikTok's short-form video format allows creative businesses to showcase their products in a new and innovative way. By creating short, engaging videos, businesses can demonstrate the benefits of their products and engage with their audience in a way that is not possible through traditional advertising.

Viral potential:
TikTok is a platform where content can quickly go viral, providing businesses with the opportunity to reach a much larger audience. By creating engaging and creative content, businesses can tap into the platform's viral potential and increase their reach.
Build brand identity: TikTok provides businesses with a platform to showcase their brand identity and create a cohesive and visually appealing brand. By curating your content and creating a unique style, businesses can create a strong brand identity that resonates with their audience.

Tips for Maximizing Your Impact on TikTok:

Create engaging content: The key to success on TikTok is to create engaging and creative content. Use the platform's unique features such as filters, effects, and music to create content that stands out and engages your audience.

Participate in challenges:

TikTok challenges are a popular feature on the platform and a great way to increase your reach and engage with your audience. By participating in relevant challenges, businesses can tap into the viral potential of the platform and reach a larger audience.

Collaborate with influencers: Influencer marketing is a powerful way to reach a broader audience and build brand awareness on TikTok. Partner with influencers in your industry to promote your products and increase your reach. Use hashtags: Hashtags are a powerful tool to increase the reach of your content and connect with your target audience. Use relevant hashtags in your videos to increase your visibility and reach new followers.

Engage with your audience: Engage with your audience by responding to comments and messages, and sharing user-generated content. By building a relationship with your audience, you can create a loyal following and increase brand awareness.

Use TikTok Ads: TikTok Ads are a powerful tool to reach a broader audience and promote your business. Use targeting features such as demographics, interests, and behaviors to create ads that reach your target audience.

In conclusion, TikTok is an essential platform for creative businesses to showcase their products and engage with their audience. By following the tips mentioned above, businesses can maximize their impact on the platform and grow their business. With its viral potential and large audience, TikTok provides a unique opportunity for creative businesses to reach a new and engaged audience.

YouTube

YouTube is the world's largest video-sharing platform with over 2 billion monthly active users. With the rise of online video consumption, YouTube has become an essential platform for creative businesses to showcase their products and services, build a following, and connect with their audience. In this article, we will explore the importance of YouTube for creative businesses and share some tips for maximizing your impact on the platform.

Why is YouTube Important for Creative Businesses?
YouTube has a massive audience: YouTube has over 2 billion active users, providing a huge potential audience for creative businesses. With the platform's global reach, businesses can reach a diverse audience that spans across different regions and demographics.

Showcase products in a detailed and engaging way: YouTube's video format allows creative businesses to showcase their products and services in a more detailed and engaging way than other platforms. By creating high-quality videos, businesses can demonstrate the benefits of their products and services and engage with their audience in a way that is not possible through traditional advertising.

Build a loyal following:
By creating regular content, businesses can build a loyal following on YouTube. Through consistent and quality content, businesses can create a connection with their audience, establish a voice, and build a community around their brand.

Monetize content:
YouTube provides businesses with an opportunity to monetize their content through advertising revenue and sponsored content. This can be a significant source of revenue for creative businesses, making it an important platform for those looking to monetize their content.

Tips for Maximizing Your Impact on YouTube:
Create high-quality and engaging content: The key to success on YouTube is to create high-quality and engaging content that resonates with your audience.

Use a professional camera and lighting, edit your videos with care, and make sure your content is both informative and entertaining.

Optimize your videos for SEO:
YouTube is the second-largest search engine in the world, so it's important to optimize your videos for search. Use relevant keywords in your video titles, descriptions, and tags to help your videos rank higher in search results. Collaborate with other creators: Collaborating with other creators is an effective way to reach a new audience and build relationships within your industry. By working with others, you can cross-promote your content, share expertise, and create new and engaging content for your audience.

Use annotations and end screens: Annotations and end screens are powerful tools that allow you to promote your other videos, channels, and merchandise within your videos. Use them to keep your audience engaged and encourage them to explore your other content.

Engage with your audience: Engage with your audience by responding to comments and messages, and encouraging user-generated content. By building a relationship with your audience, you can create a loyal following and increase brand awareness.

Promote your videos on other platforms: Promote your videos on other social media platforms, such as Twitter, Facebook, and Instagram, to increase your reach and promote your brand.

In conclusion, YouTube is an essential platform for creative businesses to showcase their products and services, build a following, and monetize their content.

By following the tips mentioned above, businesses can maximize their impact on the platform and grow their business. With its massive audience and video format, YouTube provides a unique opportunity for creative businesses to showcase their brand, engage with their audience, and grow their business.

Running an art business can be challenging, and there may be times when the going gets tough. Here are some tips to help you continue your art business during tough times:

1. Evaluate your business: Take a close look at your business and identify areas where you can cut costs or improve efficiency. Consider things like marketing expenses, inventory management, and staffing costs.

2. Diversify your revenue streams: Explore new ways to generate revenue for your business. This could involve offering new products or services, collaborating with other artists, or exploring new sales channels.

3. Connect with your community: Reach out to your local community and build relationships with other artists, businesses, and potential customers. Attend local events, join artist groups, and network with other artists and art lovers.

4. Use social media: Social media can be a powerful tool for artists to connect with potential customers and promote their work. Consider investing time and resources in building a strong social media presence.

5. Stay positive and flexible: It's important to stay positive and flexible during tough times. Be open to new ideas and opportunities, and don't be afraid to pivot your business model if needed.

6. Take care of yourself: Running a business during tough times can be stressful, so it's important to take care of yourself. Make sure to prioritize self-care and find ways to manage stress, whether that's through exercise, meditation, or other means. Remember, tough times are a part of running any business, and it's important to stay resilient and adaptable in order to overcome them. With hard work and determination, you can continue to grow your art business even during challenging times.

Chapter 7 - Copywriting your content.

Copyrighting your creative materials is an important step towards protecting your intellectual property. Whether you are a writer, artist, musician, or filmmaker, copyrighting ensures that your work is protected from unauthorized use and exploitation. In this article, we will discuss the basics of copyrighting your creative materials, including what copyright is, what can be copyrighted, the benefits of copyrighting your work, and how to go about the copyrighting process.

What is Copyright?

Copyright is a form of legal protection that grants the creator of an original work exclusive rights over its use and distribution. Copyright applies to a wide range of creative materials, including literary works, visual arts, music, and film. Copyright protection is automatic and begins as soon as the work is created, without the need for registration or other formalities.

The rights granted to the copyright holder include the right to reproduce the work, prepare derivative works based on the original, distribute copies of the work to the public, and perform or display the work publicly. Copyright also grants the holder the right to license the work to others for use, and to receive compensation for such use.

What Can be Copyrighted?

Copyright applies to a wide range of creative materials, including:

Literary works, such as books, articles, poems, and computer software.

Visual arts, such as paintings, drawings, photographs, and sculptures.

Music and sound recordings, including songs, instrumental music, and audio recordings.

Film and video, including movies, TV shows, and documentaries.

Architecture, including buildings and other structures.

In order to be eligible for copyright protection, the work must be original and fixed in a tangible medium of expression. This means that the work must be the product of the author's original creative effort, and must be in a form that can be perceived, reproduced, or otherwise communicated. Ideas, concepts, and methods cannot be copyrighted, only the expression of those ideas.

Benefits of Copyrighting Your Work:
There are several benefits to copyrighting your creative materials, including:
Protection from unauthorized use - Copyright protection ensures that others cannot use or exploit your work without your permission. This includes copying, distributing, performing, or displaying your work in public.
Ability to license your work - Copyright gives you the right to license your work to others for use. This can provide a source of income through licensing fees or royalties.

Enforcement of your rights - Copyright provides legal recourse in case someone infringes on your rights. If someone uses your work without your permission, you can take legal action to stop them and seek damages.
Increased value - Copyright protection can increase the value of your work. This is particularly true for commercial works, such as music or film, where copyright is an essential part of the economic value of the work.

How to Copyright Your Creative Materials

The copyrighting process varies depending on the type of work you are seeking to protect. In general, however, there are three basic steps to copyrighting your creative materials:

Step 1: Create the Work
The first step in copyrighting your work is to create it. The work must be original and fixed in a tangible medium of expression. This means that you must have created the work yourself, and it must exist in a form that can be perceived, reproduced, or communicated.

Step 2: Register the Copyright
The next step in copyrighting your work is to register it with the copyright office. While copyright protection is automatic, registering your work provides additional legal protection and establishes a public record of your ownership. You can register your work with the U.S. Copyright Office online, by mail, or in person. The registration process typically involves filling out an application form, paying a fee, and submitting a copy of the work being registered.

Step 3: Monitor and Enforce Your Rights

Once you have registered your copyright, it is important to monitor and enforce your rights. This involves keeping an eye out for unauthorized use or infringement of your work, and taking legal action if necessary.

Some steps you can take to monitor and enforce your rights include:

Keeping track of where your work is being used or distributed, and whether or not you have given permission for that use.

Using copyright notices on your work, such as the © symbol and your name or the year of creation, to indicate your ownership and rights.

Conducting regular online searches for your work, to identify any unauthorized uses or infringements.

Sending cease-and-desist letters to anyone using your work without permission, and taking legal action if necessary.

Seeking the help of a lawyer or legal professional to assist you in enforcing your rights.

Tips for Copyrighting Your Creative Materials

Here are some additional tips to keep in mind when copyrighting your creative materials:

Consider using a copyright attorney - If you have complex copyright issues or questions, it may be helpful to consult with a copyright attorney who can guide you through the process.

Keep detailed records - It is important to keep detailed records of when and how your work was created, as well as any licenses or permissions you have granted.

Be mindful of fair use - While copyright protection is important, it is also important to recognize the concept of fair use. Fair use allows for limited use of copyrighted material for purposes such as criticism, comment, news reporting, teaching, scholarship, or research. Understanding the concept of fair use can help you avoid unnecessary legal disputes.

Consider international copyright protection - If your work will be distributed internationally, it may be beneficial to seek copyright protection in other countries as well.

Conclusion

Copyrighting your creative materials is an important step towards protecting your intellectual property and ensuring that your work is not exploited without your permission. By understanding the basics of copyright law and taking the necessary steps to register and monitor your copyright, you can safeguard your work and enjoy the benefits of copyright protection. Remember to keep detailed records, be mindful of fair use, and seek the help of a copyright attorney if necessary. With these tips in mind, you can successfully copyright your creative materials and enjoy the peace of mind that comes with knowing your work is protected.

Chapter 8 - Any other things I can think of to help you...

How to deal with difficult customers...

Dealing with difficult customers can be a challenge, but it's an inevitable part of running a business. Here are some tips to help you handle difficult customers:

1. Listen actively: Listen carefully to the customer's concerns and try to understand their perspective. Acknowledge their feelings and let them know that you're taking their concerns seriously.

2. Stay calm and professional: Don't take the customer's behaviour personally, and avoid getting defensive or argumentative. Stay calm and professional, and focus on finding a solution to their problem.

3. Apologize and take responsibility: If you or your business has made a mistake, apologize and take responsibility. This can help to defuse the situation and show the customer that you're willing to make things right.

4. Offer a solution: Work with the customer to find a solution to their problem. This may involve offering a refund, a replacement, or another form of compensation.

5. Know when to walk away: If the customer is being abusive or unreasonable, it's okay to set boundaries and end the conversation. It's important to prioritize your own mental health and wellbeing. By following these tips, you can effectively manage difficult customers and maintain a positive relationship with your clients. Remember, even difficult customers can be an opportunity to learn and improve your business practices. how to develop the discipline to do what needs to be done Developing discipline can be challenging, but it's an essential skill for achieving your goals and being productive.

Keeping the fires burning...

Creative passions are essential for personal growth and development, and can be a source of joy and fulfilment in our lives. However, it can be challenging to keep our creative passions alive amidst the demands and stresses of daily life. In this article, we will explore some practical ways to keep our creative passions alive and thriving.

Make Time for Creativity
One of the most important things we can do to keep our creative passions alive is to make time for them. This means setting aside regular time in our schedules for creative activities, whether that be writing, painting, playing music, or any other creative pursuit.
It can be helpful to schedule this time in advance and treat it as a non-negotiable commitment. This can help us prioritize our creative passions and ensure that we are giving them the time and attention they deserve.

Embrace Imperfection
Another key to keeping our creative passions alive is to embrace imperfection. Creative endeavours can be challenging and often involve a great deal of trial and error. It is important to remember that mistakes and failures are a natural part of the creative process and can actually be valuable learning opportunities.
Rather than striving for perfection, it can be helpful to focus on the process of creation itself and enjoy the journey. This can help us stay motivated and inspired, even when things don't turn out exactly as we had hoped.

Experiment and Explore
To keep our creative passions alive, it is important to stay curious and open to new ideas and experiences. This means experimenting with new techniques, materials, and approaches to our creative pursuits.
Taking the time to explore new ideas and approaches can help us stay inspired and engaged with our creative passions. It can also help us develop new skills and perspectives that can enrich our creative work.

Seek Out Inspiration
Inspiration is essential for keeping our creative passions alive, and there are many ways to seek it out. This might involve reading books, watching movies

or TV shows, attending live performances or events, or simply taking a walk-in nature.

It can also be helpful to seek out the work of other artists and creatives, whether that be through social media, art galleries, or online communities. Seeing the work of others can help us stay motivated and inspired, and can also help us learn new techniques and approaches to our own creative work.

Collaborate with Others

Collaboration can be a powerful way to keep our creative passions alive. Working with others can help us stay motivated and inspired, and can also help us develop new skills and perspectives.

This might involve collaborating with other artists or creatives on a project, or simply sharing our work with friends and family for feedback and support. Collaborating with others can also help us build a sense of community and belonging around our creative passions.

Take Breaks and Rest

Finally, it is important to remember that rest and relaxation are essential for keeping our creative passions alive. Burnout and exhaustion can quickly sap our creative energy and motivation, so it is important to take breaks and give ourselves time to recharge.

This might involve taking a day off from creative work, going for a walk in nature, or simply taking a nap. By prioritizing rest and self-care, we can ensure that our creative passions remain a source of joy and inspiration in our lives.

Conclusion

Keeping our creative passions alive requires dedication, curiosity, and a willingness to embrace imperfection and experimentation. By making time for creativity, seeking out inspiration, collaborating with others, and prioritizing rest and relaxation, we can ensure that our creative passions remain a vibrant and essential part of our lives.

Why building an email list is vital...

In today's digital age, email marketing remains one of the most effective ways to reach and engage with customers. An email list is a crucial component of any email marketing campaign, as it allows businesses and organizations to connect with their audience in a more personal and targeted way. In this article, we will explore the importance of building an email list and provide some tips for creating a successful email marketing strategy.

What is an Email List?

An email list is a collection of email addresses that businesses and organizations use to send marketing messages and updates to their subscribers. An email list can include existing customers, website visitors, social media followers, and anyone else who has opted-in to receive communications from the business.

Why is Building an Email List Important?

Reach a Targeted Audience

Unlike other forms of digital marketing, such as social media or search engine advertising, email marketing allows businesses to reach a highly targeted audience. By building an email list of subscribers who have expressed interest in the business or its products, businesses can ensure that their marketing messages are reaching the people who are most likely to engage with them.

Cost-Effective Marketing

Email marketing is a highly cost-effective way to reach and engage with customers. Unlike traditional advertising methods, such as print or television ads, email marketing requires only minimal investment in terms of time and resources. Once a business has built a list of email subscribers, it can send marketing messages to them at virtually no cost.

Increased Engagement and Conversion Rates

Email marketing is one of the most effective ways to drive engagement and conversions. According to a study by Campaign Monitor, email marketing has a median ROI of 122%, which is four times higher than other marketing formats, including social media and direct mail.

Build Relationships and Trust

Email marketing allows businesses to build relationships and trust with their subscribers. By sending personalized and relevant messages, businesses can demonstrate their expertise and knowledge, and establish themselves as a trusted source of information and advice.

Control Over Marketing Messages

Email marketing gives businesses complete control over their marketing messages. Unlike social media or search engine advertising, where algorithms determine who sees a particular message, businesses can be sure that their email marketing messages are reaching their intended audience.

Tips for Building an Email List

Provide Value

The key to building a successful email list is to provide value to your subscribers. This can include offering exclusive discounts or promotions, providing helpful tips and advice, or sharing relevant news and updates. By providing value to your subscribers, you can build trust and establish yourself as a trusted source of information and advice in your industry.

Use Opt-In Forms

Opt-in forms are a crucial tool for building an email list. These forms allow visitors to your website to sign up for your email list by providing their name and email address.

To maximize the effectiveness of your opt-in forms, make sure they are prominently displayed on your website and offer a clear and compelling incentive for visitors to sign up.

Segment Your List

Segmenting your email list allows you to send more personalized and targeted messages to your subscribers. By dividing your list into different segments based on factors such as location, interests, or purchase history, you can send more relevant messages that are more likely to resonate with your subscribers.

Test and Experiment

As with any marketing strategy, it is important to test and experiment with different approaches to see what works best. This might involve testing different subject lines, sending times, or calls to action to see what generates the most engagement and conversions.

By continually testing and experimenting, you can refine your email marketing strategy over time and ensure that you are delivering the most effective messages to your subscribers.

Nurture Your Subscribers

Building an email list is just the first step in a successful email marketing strategy. By sending regular and relevant messages that provide value and build trust a company can set itself apart from the competition.

This can involve a variety of tactics, including:

Welcome Emails: When someone first signs up for your email list, send them a welcome email that thanks them for joining and provides them with more information about your business and what they can expect from your emails.

Segmented Content: As mentioned earlier, segmenting your email list allows you to send more personalized messages that are tailored to each subscriber's interests and preferences.

Promotions and Offers: Offering exclusive discounts or promotions to your email subscribers is a great way to keep them engaged and encourage them to make a purchase.

Educational Content: Providing educational content, such as how-to guides, industry news, or expert advice, is a great way to establish your business as a thought leader and build trust with your subscribers.

Event Invitations: If your business hosts events or webinars, make sure to invite your email subscribers to attend. This is a great way to build relationships with your subscribers and provide them with additional value.

Surveys and Feedback Requests: Asking for feedback from your email subscribers can help you better understand their needs and preferences, and tailor your marketing messages accordingly.

Consistent Communication: Finally, it is important to maintain consistent communication with your email subscribers. This means sending regular messages on a consistent schedule, and avoiding long periods of inactivity that can cause subscribers to lose interest.

Conclusion

Building an email list is a crucial component of any successful email marketing strategy. By providing value to your subscribers, segmenting your list, testing and experimenting with different approaches, and nurturing your subscribers with regular and relevant messages, you can establish yourself as a trusted source of information and advice in your industry, and drive engagement and conversions for your business.

Be disciplined in getting things done...

Here are some tips to help you develop the discipline to do what needs to be done:
1. Set clear goals: Start by setting clear, measurable goals for yourself. This will give you a sense of purpose and help you stay focused on what you need to do.

2.Create a schedule: Make a schedule or a to-do list to help you prioritize your tasks and stay on track. This will help you avoid procrastination and make the most of your time.

3. Break tasks into smaller steps: If a task feels overwhelming, try breaking it down into smaller, more manageable steps. This can help you feel less intimidated and make progress more easily.

4. Find an accountability partner: Consider finding an accountability partner, someone who can hold you accountable for completing your tasks and help keep you on track.

5. Practice self-care: Taking care of yourself physically and mentally can help you build the resilience and motivation you need to stay disciplined. This may involve getting enough sleep, eating well, and engaging in regular exercise.

6. Celebrate your successes: Celebrate your accomplishments, no matter how small they may seem. This can help you stay motivated and build momentum towards your goals. By implementing these strategies and staying focused on your goals, you can develop the discipline to do what needs to be done and achieve the success you are looking for.

Being productive is crucial for achieving success in both personal and professional pursuits. However, it can often be challenging to maintain focus and consistently produce high-quality work. In this article, we will explore various strategies for maximizing productivity and achieving your goals.

Set Clear Goals

The first step in becoming more productive is to set clear and achievable goals. Without specific objectives, it can be challenging to maintain focus and direction. Begin by identifying what you want to accomplish and why it is important. Then, break down larger goals into smaller, more manageable tasks that can be completed on a daily or weekly basis.

Prioritize Your Tasks

Once you have identified your goals, it is essential to prioritize your tasks to ensure that you are making progress towards your objectives. One effective method for prioritizing tasks is to use the Eisenhower Matrix. This matrix involves dividing tasks into four categories: urgent and important, important but not urgent, urgent but not important, and neither urgent nor important. By focusing on tasks that are both urgent and important, you can ensure that you are making progress towards your goals.

Create a Schedule

Creating a schedule is an effective way to manage your time and ensure that you are maximizing productivity. Begin by identifying the most important tasks that need to be completed each day and schedule them during your most productive hours. Additionally, be sure to schedule breaks and downtime to avoid burnout and maintain focus throughout the day.

Eliminate Distractions

Distractions can significantly impact productivity and prevent you from accomplishing your goals. Some common distractions include social media, email notifications, and irrelevant conversations. To minimize distractions, consider implementing the following strategies:
Turn off notifications on your phone or computer.
Use website blockers to prevent access to distracting websites.
Schedule specific times to check email and social media.

Communicate your need for uninterrupted work time to co-workers and family members.

Manage Your Energy

Maximizing productivity requires not only managing your time but also managing your energy levels. This involves identifying the times of day when you are most productive and scheduling your most important tasks during those times. Additionally, be sure to prioritize self-care activities, such as exercise, healthy eating, and getting enough sleep, to maintain high levels of energy and focus throughout the day.

Take Breaks

Taking regular breaks is crucial for maintaining focus and avoiding burnout. Research suggests that taking short breaks every 90 minutes can significantly improve productivity and reduce stress. During breaks, consider engaging in activities that help you recharge, such as stretching, going for a walk, or practicing mindfulness.

Use Technology to Your Advantage

Technology can be a valuable tool for maximizing productivity. Some useful technologies include:

Time-tracking apps: These apps can help you identify how you are spending your time and make adjustments to improve productivity.

Productivity apps: These apps can help you manage tasks, schedule appointments, and stay organized.

Virtual assistants: Virtual assistants can help you manage administrative tasks, freeing up time for more important work.

Focus on One Task at a Time

Multitasking can often be counterproductive, as it can reduce focus and increase the likelihood of errors. Instead, focus on one task at a time, completing it before moving on to the next. This approach can improve concentration and allow you to complete tasks more efficiently.

Use the Pomodoro Technique

The Pomodoro Technique is a time-management strategy that involves working in focused 25-minute intervals, followed by a 5-minute break. After completing four Pomodoro cycles, take a more extended 15-minute break.

This technique can help improve productivity by breaking down work into manageable chunks and providing regular opportunities for rest and rejuvenation.

Embrace Continuous Learning

Continuously learning and developing new skills is an important aspect of productivity. By expanding your knowledge and skills, you can improve your ability to complete tasks efficiently and effectively. Additionally, learning new things can keep you engaged and motivated, preventing burnout and boredom.

Here are some strategies for embracing continuous learning:

Set Learning Goals

To ensure that you are continuously learning, set specific learning goals that align with your personal and professional objectives. This could include learning a new programming language, developing a new skill, or earning a certification in your field.

Attend Workshops and Conferences

Attending workshops and conferences is an excellent way to gain new insights and learn from experts in your field. These events provide opportunities to network with others, ask questions, and participate in hands-on learning experiences.

Read Books and Articles

Reading books and articles is an effective way to stay informed about the latest trends and best practices in your field. Additionally, reading can help you expand your knowledge and develop critical thinking skills.

Take Online Courses

Online courses are an excellent way to learn new skills and gain knowledge in a flexible and convenient format. Many online courses are self-paced, allowing you to learn at your own pace and on your own schedule.

Participate in Skill-Sharing Communities

Participating in skill-sharing communities, such as forums, online groups, or in-person meetups, can provide opportunities to learn from others and share your own knowledge and experiences.

Learn from Mentors

Finding a mentor who can provide guidance and support can be an invaluable way to learn new skills and develop professionally. Mentors can provide insights into your field, offer feedback on your work, and provide encouragement and support as you grow.

Practice Continuous Reflection

Reflecting on your work and learning experiences is a valuable way to identify areas for improvement and continue to develop your skills. This could include journaling, discussing your experiences with colleagues or mentors, or seeking feedback from others.

Overall, continuous learning is an essential component of productivity. By embracing new opportunities for learning and development, you can improve your ability to complete tasks efficiently and effectively, stay motivated, and achieve your goals.

To conclude this book,

I want to end with a few final words of encouragement for you and your family.

The best way to help a creative mind will depend on the individual and their unique needs and goals. However, here are some general tips that may be helpful:

1. Encourage their creativity: Let the creative person in your life know that you value their creativity and encourage them to pursue their passions. Offer positive feedback and support, and help them find ways to develop their skills.

2. Create a positive environment: Provide a safe and positive environment for the creative person to explore their ideas and express themselves. This may involve creating a dedicated workspace or providing the tools and resources they need to create.

3. Respect their process: Recognize that creativity can be messy and unpredictable, and try to respect the creative person's process. Avoid pressuring them to meet specific deadlines or work in a certain way, and instead give them the freedom to explore and experiment.

4. Collaborate with them: Consider collaborating with the creative person on a project or offering to provide feedback on their work. This can help them stay motivated and inspired, and may lead to new creative ideas.

5. Help them find opportunities: Look for ways to help the creative person find opportunities to share their work and connect with other creative individuals. This may involve networking, attending events, or seeking out opportunities for exhibitions or performances. By providing support, encouragement, and opportunities, you can help a creative mind to thrive and reach their full potential.

About the Author...

About the Author About the author Over the years, I have got to know John, not just as an artist, but as my best friend and husband. I have seen him at his best and definitely at his worst. I've gone through it all with him and it has been a wonderful journey. I'd like to share with you a little of the story so far.

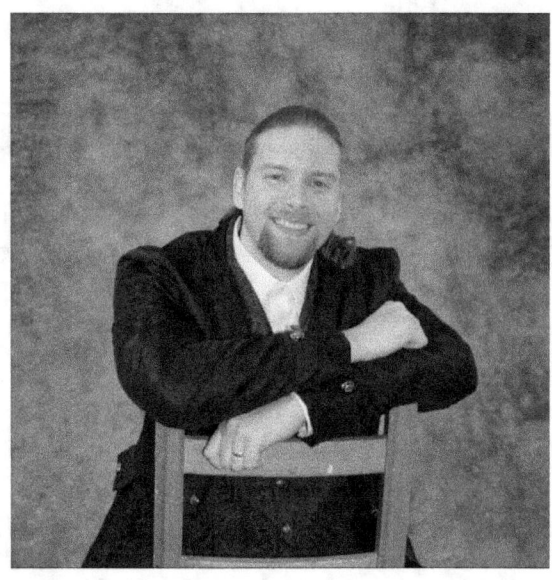

John was born in Huddersfield, West Yorkshire, in 1988. April 3rd to be exact. Over the next 21 years, John remained in Huddersfield at home with his parents. During this time, he began to follow his passions for bodybuilding, wrestling, music, youth work and eventually, his true love, art. John applied himself fully to his passions, winning awards in bodybuilding, learning to play guitar beautifully, becoming passionate about the lives of others and developing his skills with a paintbrush.

Sadly, during John's biggest accomplishments in bodybuilding, he took ill and was diagnosed with Ulcerative Colitis; a debilitating condition that attacks the immune system and intestine. However, John has always had an interesting way of looking at things and whereas many would give up or limit themselves, John felt that, regardless of his diagnosis, he was going to leave his mark on the world. It was around this time, when John turned on the TV and landed on a programme that would change his life forever. A ginger, afro-haired man by the name of Bob Ross appeared on the T.V: A world-famous teacher on how to paint, John became mesmerised and fell in love with art and Bob Ross. John found brushes and paper and began painting and learning his techniques.

Through the struggles and trials of the learning process, he never gave up and began to develop his own style. I especially love his mountain and seascapes as they evoke the true heart of John on canvas. They are just beautiful. John's unique approach to life and people opened up the opportunity to work with youth.

This eventually brought John to Scotland where he took up the position of Youth Pastor with a local Church of Scotland. He built up a youth group that was a mixture of youth who attended the Church, and those from the surrounding community. It was the community youth that John found a particular affinity with and expended great energy on making them feel valued and a part of something worthwhile. John got the opportunity to include his art skills with the youth group which incorporated the chance to voice their views on God, life, and society while they learned a new skill. The duo aspect of the activity created a safe place for attendees to be who they were and express themselves.

 One of John's greatest gifts is the ability to listen and ask the right questions at the right time, a gift that John not only put to good use here but has used all through his adult life to help and reach people from all walks of life. In 2011 John began taking jobs as an illustrator with authors Cindy Freland, Anna Renault, Latoya Williams, and Yvette Albury, among others. In 2013, an amazing opportunity to travel to the USA on tour with his art business presented itself. 94 His dear friend, the late Anna Renault, organised and hosted John on this trip, forging a lasting friendship that I know he will always treasure. During this amazing time, he was brought back down to earth with a bang as his landlord and "best friend" decided to evict John whilst still on tour. On his return to Scotland, he found his whole life had been packed up and left in a terrible bedsit. The turmoil that John felt during this time affected him deeply and has taken many years to work through. John spent eight months in the bedsit, a difficult period of time that was punctuated with, I hope, an incredibly happy occurrence. He met me! At the end of the eight months, determined to fight onward, yet feeling fundamentally changed by this, and other experiences, John moved into his own flat.

The pressures of life changed John, but thankfully, he never lost that wonderful spirit and drive for life. I have never met anyone who has the self-discipline that John has. It drives me nuts sometimes! By May 2014, John and I were engaged! Life has a funny way of throwing curve balls, as Anna Renault used to often say. I have seen him ill with Amaurosis, Dyspraxia and Colitis and many other health complaints and yet his determination to succeed paved the way for him to build a full-time art business where he could work from home. When our usual means of income became fruitless because of marketing changes on Facebook, John built an Art School reaching over 45 students. He has literally gone from having almost nothing, to being able to buy our first home. It has been such a journey and I invite you to share the journey with us as we continue our adventure through life. This book which you are holding in your hands, has launched a brand-new branch to our business called Mind, Body & Soul. It seeks to encourage, motivate, and inspire you through the craziness of day-to-day life and put that spring back into your step. There is so much more to his story and one day if you are lucky, he may just share with you a chapter or two. Katie

Taking things further...

We hope you have enjoyed this book and found it helpful.
If you have and if you have implemented the contents within, then you are 90% further on than the rest of the global population.
Most buy these things and never read them, or if they read them they fail to take action on the actual doing of each and every task.

John coaches' creative minds around the world. He ain't cheap but he is good. Working with John will ensure your creative business the best chance of its success. John has coaching sessions available in the form of 1 on 1 coaching and group coaching, all of which take place online and weekly.
If this would be of interest to you then just click the link
here https://thejohnmorris.co.uk/creative_business_builder/
Also, If coaching isn't for you and you would rather do things step by step in your own time, then why not check out John's courses. From building a successful creative business, writing your first novel to building a 100% optimised and easy to use website John has created those courses especially for you and creative minds around the world just like you.
One final thing...
If you did enjoy this book then please a) leave a positive review on amazon or our website and b) tell your creative friends about it, encourage them to pick up a copy of their own. Doing this helps our little business continue to grow

and thrive and ensures that we can continue teaching and helping other creative minds around the world.

So, if this is where our journey ends, then we wish you all of life's blessings and all the very best with your creative endeavours. If not, and you are ready to take things further, then come aboard the train to success, take your seat and let's begin this exciting journey together.

Visit https://thejohnmorris.co.uk/creative_business_builder/ for more information.